Animal A-Z

Written by Louisa Cornford
Designed by Bethany Side
and Nicola Friggens

priddy books
big ideas for little people

Found in parts of Central and **South America**, **anteaters** are known for their long, bushy tails and very thin snouts. They shuffle about on their knuckles and break open **ant nests** with their claws. Anteaters can flick their **tongues** over 160 times a minute.

Anteaters have bad eyesight, but a very good sense of smell

A is for Anteater

B is for Bear

Thick, hairy coat

Good sense of smell

These large meat-eating **mammals** are found in parts of Europe, Asia, **America** and north Africa. Brown bears are the biggest type of bear. Most bears have a huge body, big **paws,** stumpy legs and a small tail. They have long claws and strong **teeth** for chewing their food.

Big paws

Thick coat for cold desert nights

Bushy eyelashes protect eyes from sand

These hump-backed mammals live in **deserts,** where they have adapted to survive the extreme climate. Their **humps** are filled with **fat** so they can last up to four days without **water.** There are very few camels left in the wild, but people still use them as a means of **transport.**

C is for Camel

Average height: 7 ft (2.1 m)

Two-toed feet

D is for Dugong

Dugongs are large marine mammals with paddle-shaped **flippers,** tusk-like teeth and a forked tail. They can be found from Africa to **Australia** in warm, shallow water, such as bays and harbors. Dugongs like to eat seagrass.

Small eyes

Bristled snout for finding food

Average length:
9 ft (2.7 m)

E is for Elephant

Elephants have long **trunks,** two tusks and big ears. They are the largest living land animals. They are found in many places, from the plains of Africa to Asian forests, where the mothers and young live in **herds,** like cows.

Thick, wrinkly skin

Elephants squirt water into their mouths with their trunks

Average height:
10 ft (3.1 m)

These bright pink wading birds have very long legs and large, downturned bills. They are found in warm water areas all over the world, where they live in groups called colonies of up to a million flamingos.

The food that they eat makes them pink

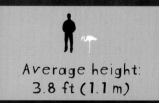

Average height: 3.8 ft (1.1 m)

Nobody knows why flamingos stand on one leg

F is for Flamingo

G is for

These large apes have thick black hair, long arms and a large forehead. Gorillas can be found in the mountains and tropical lowlands of Africa. They are thought to be very clever — their closest relatives are humans and chimpanzees.

Gorilla

Longer arms than legs

This is a silverback gorilla

Average height 5 ft (1.5 m)

Average length:
12 ft (3.7 m)

Hippos live in large groups near rivers, swamps and lakes in Africa. These huge mammals wallow in water and mud and graze on grass. Although they have large bodies with stumpy legs, hippos are able to **run** faster than humans.

Hippos bathe in mud and water to keep their skin cool and moist

H is for Hippopotamus

I is for

Impalas are small antelopes that live in the **grasslands** of Africa. They are able to run very quickly, leaping distances of over 33 feet (10 m) to escape fast **predators** such as hyenas, cheetahs and lions.

Male impalas have very long, spiral horns

Small, slim body means they can run away easily

Average height: 35 in (89 cm)

Impala

J is for Jaguar

Jaguars can be found in South and Central America. Unlike most **cats,** they do not mind water and are good **swimmers,** catching prey such as turtles in rivers. Although similar in appearance to a leopard, their **markings** are larger, with dark **spots** in the middle.

Spotted coat to hide among trees

Powerful jaw muscles crack open tough turtle shells

Average length
5.5 ft (1.7 m)

K is for Koala

Average height:
38 in (97 cm)

Sharp claws for climbing trees

Koalas are gray marsupials with short, thick fur, sharp claws and tufty ears. Found in Australia, they eat lots of eucalyptus and spend most of their time asleep up trees. Baby koalas are called joeys.

These wide-eyed, long-tailed **primates** are found only on Madagascar, an island off the east coast of Africa. They have a pointed face like a fox and live in groups in rocky **scrub** and rainforest areas. There are nearly 100 types of lemur and they all look slightly different.

Lemurs eat flowers, insects, fruit, leaves and tree gum

This is a ring-tailed lemur

L is for Lemur

Average length: 18 in (46 cm)

This is a hyacinth macaw

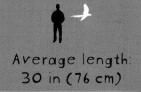

Average length:
30 in (76 cm)

Sharp beak to crack open seeds

M is for Macaw

Macaws are large **parrots** that live in South America. They have long tails, bright, colorful feathers, and can be found in tropical forests. They feed on fruit, seeds, flowers and nuts. Macaws can **screech** very loudly.

N is for Narwhal

The male's tusk can grow up to 10 feet (3 m)

Narwhals eat fish, squid and shrimp

Average length: 15 ft (4.6 m)

Found in river and coastal areas of the Arctic, these unusual looking whales have long, mottled bodies, little fins and a large mouth with only two teeth. Male narwhals are easily identified, as one tooth grows into a long, sword-like tusk.

O is for

Red-brown fur

Average height:
5 ft (1.5 m)

Very long arms

These **red-brown** apes live only in the **rainforests** of Asia, where they **swing** through the trees with their long arms. The diet of an **orangutan** is mainly made up of sweet foods, like **fruit**, shoots, honey and bird's eggs.

Orangutan

Giant **pandas** live in the **mountains** of central China. They like to climb trees and feed on **bamboo** shoots. These bears are well-known for their **black** and **white** fur. Pandas are endangered due to their limited diet and **hunting.**

Average length:
4 ft (1.2 m)

Cat-like eyes

Black eye patches

P is for Panda

Q is for

This is a resplendent quetzal

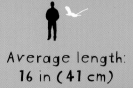
Mixture of green, blue and red feathers

This brightly-colored quetzal is one of the most beautiful birds in the world. An endangered animal, it lives in the mountainous tropical forests of Central America. It is also the national symbol for Guatemala — the country has even named its currency after the bird!

Quetzal

Male tail feathers grow up to 25 inches (64 cm)

R is for Rhinoceros

Both male and female rhinos have horns

Average length: 12 ft (3.7 m)

Thick, plate-like skin

This white rhino is the largest of the five species

Rhinos are **huge** and can weigh as much as 2,200 pounds (4,000 kg). A **rhino** has one or two horns, depending on its species. These horns are made of a tough material called keratin. Sadly, they are endangered and not many remain in the wild.

S is for Sloth

Long claws to hang from branches

Found in the **tropical** forests of South and Central America, these **furry** mammals are known for being very slow and sleepy. They **hang** upside down from the tops of trees and blend in with the branches to avoid predators.

Red-brown fur

Average length: 20 in (51 cm)

The largest big cat in the world, the carnivorous tiger lives in the rainforests, mountains and grasslands of parts of Asia and Russia. They have orange and white fur with a distinctive pattern of black stripes which helps them to hide.

Excellent eyesight

Striped fur

Average length:
10 ft (3.5 m)

T is for Tiger

U is for

This **black-feathered** bird is named for the **striking** crest of feathers on its head. It lives in the tropical **forests** of South and Central America. The all-black appearance of the **umbrella bird** is **unusual** for a tropical bird — normally they are very colorful.

Umbrella-like crest

Umbrella Bird

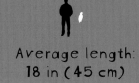

Average length: 18 in (45 cm)

There are 22 types of vultures, found on every continent except Antarctica and Australia. These large, meat-eating birds fill up on food when they can, so that they can go for long periods without eating.

This is a griffon vulture

Average length 3.3 ft (1 m)

Fluffy feathers

Very good eyesight

V is for Vulture

These **bulky,** flippered mammals live in the Arctic.
They spend most of their time in the icy water
and have a **thick** layer of fat, called **blubber**
to keep them warm in the extreme cold.
All walruses have long **tusks** and
bristly whiskers, but female
tusks are slightly shorter.

Small, beady
eyes

Long tusks

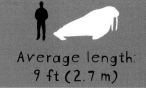

Average length:
9 ft (2.7 m)

W is for Walrus

X is for X-ray Fish

Silver, sparkling body

These **sparkling** fish are very **small** and unusual. They are called x-ray fish because of their **shiny**, almost **see-through** bodies. They live in the coastal rivers of South America, where they **swim** around in big groups and like to feed on small insects and **plankton**.

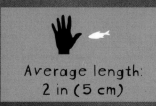

Average length:
2 in (5 cm)

Y is for Yak

Average length:
10.5 ft (3.2 m)

Long horns

Tall shoulders

Yaks are **bulky,** hairy mammals that live in the mountains of south and southeast Asia. Their long, shaggy hair is white, brown or black and perfect for protecting them from the **cold.** They chew on moss and grass and crunch on the **snow** when they are thirsty.

Z is for Zebra

Average length:
8 ft (2.4 m)

Each zebra has a different stripe pattern

Zebras are found in east and southern **Africa.** These fast-running, **hoofed** mammals are closely related to horses. Their **black and white** stripes are good camouflage in the long grass. Zebras like to eat grass and spend their time **grazing** in large groups.

Glossary

Camouflage Colors and patterns that help an animal blend into their surroundings.

Carnivore A meat-eating animal.

Continent Dry land on Earth is divided into seven areas, called continents. They are: Antarctica, Africa, Asia, Australia, North America, South America and Europe.

Desert Dry landscapes where there is not very much rainfall, plants or animals. An example of a large desert is the Sahara Desert.

Endangered Species of animals that are at risk of dying out are called endangered. This can be due to poaching, changes in environment or reduced numbers.

Extinct When a species of animal dies out it is extinct.

Flipper Flat, paddle-like limbs of some sea mammals.

Fin Limbs of some sea animals, used to move through water and keep them stable.

Hemisphere Earth is divided into two hemispheres — the northern and the southern hemisphere.

Herd The common collective name for a group of mammals. Other names include colonies and troops.

Horns A long, pointed growth on the head of some mammals made of keratin and bone. Some horns are hollow.